Hearing Things
and Other Arts

poems and collages

by

Carlo Levy

ATOPON BOOKS

Atopon Books
907 15th Street
Santa Monica, California 90403
United States

Library of Congress Cataloguing-in-Publication data
Names: Levy, Carlo, author.
Title: Hearing things and other arts / Carlo Levy.
Description: Santa Monica, CA: Atopon Books, 2023.
Identifiers: LCCN 2023940395 | ISBN: 979-8-9866907-7-3
Subjects: LCSH Poetry--American. | Poets--Washington
(State)--Seattle. | Collage--American | Literature and mental
illness. | BISAC POETRY / American / General | ART /
American | BIOGRAPHY AND AUTOBIOGRAPHY /
Personal Memoirs
Classification: LCC PS3562.E7756 O85 2023 | DDC 813.6--dc23

"The Newly Developed, Revolutionary Typewriter" appeared
originally in *Fine Madness*, Spring 1987

"The Old Music of Heraclitus" appeared in *Fine Madness*, 1997

"Myra and the Woman on the Stock" appeared in *Floating
Bridge Review*, 2011, after first appearing in *The Seattle Review*,
Fall 1985, in a slightly different version.

"Strange Gardens, Companions" appeared in the Appendices
of Connie Sidles' book *In My Nature: A Birder's Year at the
Montlake Fill* (2009)

Cover credit: lavender paper texture background. colored cardboard
fibers and grain. empty space concept © Adobe Stock / golubovy

Printed in the United States of America

In loving memory of my mom,
Helen Twardoski
(1925-2022)

Many thanks and great appreciation for my wife and dearest
one, Rebecca, and my dear old friends Stefan and Chris.

With special thanks to Joseph Cornell.

Table of Contents

The Old Music of Heraclitus   11

Double and Whole Vision   19

The School of Alice   23

Assignment #1 - Megalomania   28

Myra and the Woman on the Stock   32

The Archaeology of Nearby Parks   37

Assignment #2 - Conspiracy   41

The Beginning Homecare Worker   46

Strange Gardens, Companions   51

Assignment #3 - Schizophrenia and Choice   55

Transcription from the Radio   58

The Newly Developed, Revolutionary Typewriter   63

Assignment #4 - Schizophrenia and Emptiness   67

The Biography of Uncommon Longing   70

From the Paper Mills   77

The Old Music of Heraclitus

Your voices told me
quietly, I could invent privacy,
a phonograph
turning inside the hedge
where the common being lives.

The maps grow
fragile leaves of a puzzle,
seedlings of voices,
tiny chairs, twigs,
pockets in your thoughts
for my hands,
cutting out pictures,
sidewalk
and rail
for the turquoise bridge
across the canal.
I walk to the arboretum,
and up the hill
to the towers of old holly.

Pete Seeger played his banjo
until I danced and fell down,
asleep.

Then a child waved a magic wand
and I disappeared.

Where are my intuitions?
The cheeks
of olive pictures
I lost, playing
on my medicine table,
legs, sticks,
string, nests
of chemistry.
The thick records
of lonely science turn.
The earth signals
my sweet
alien, protected
by memory
of the foreign shoulders.

Where I learned
how to read books,
birds flew
to the small, wood
scale, the house
closed with seeds.

The measurement spoke
to the rain cloud,
a grey apology.

The animals around the story
and the common being I saw
told me before I fell asleep
but now I'm ashamed
of my despair,
my pillow
all of you can mark.

She is inside me,
my own friend,
looking away from me
and back inside,
revolving like a phonograph

sewing
impulses
into a dress around me,

lifting,

and she is unknown to you,

but then, I know
she is only you,
reading parts of me
stored inside,
finding another
story below,
or above.

Am I also creating you,
disappearing
in the shape of another
world?

How do we make
the invisible
shapes together,

imagining privacy
overlap?

I can't trust the beings
from the lips of the beds
to mediate in the earthly city,
invisible immigrants
closing my suitcase,
my eyes, the lid
of the simple television
filled with shells.

My phonograph sews impulses into clothes
I remove

and wear, sleeves,
branches and hands
holding fruit,
little motors ripening
in the radio of the future.

The spools listen
inside my sockets,
your eyes

inside mine,
loosening,
pulling, voices and wheels
of the archipelago.

Double and Whole Vision

A sister and brother,
my eyes began to part.
I gathered them back
to be together
but in school, blackboards
divided, the felt alphabet
fell loose.
I had chosen one eye
to look through,
saw woodwork, never the room,
one cheek mirrored,
missing a friend.

Only words swept my eyes
together to see one story.

Bees in jars,
a bicycle, a domino,
mothers, shoulders
settled and formed rooms,
yards, rocks in a river.

Off the page people separated.

Eventually even words weakened,
got doubled. A surgeon
restrung the muscles of my eyes.

I pulled my new line of eyes in,
let it fall
slanted
and my head shook,
splicing my eyes.

I saw the room I was in.
Poles and wires untangled outside
and birds flew into each other.

People embraced in a meadow,
amused to see me returning
their gaze, like an old man
laughing in a maze.

The School of Alice

The higgledy-piggledy school house
stairs go up and down, wooden, eternal
stairwells and footsteps through tunnels
in gardens of bones,
children talking about lupines
growing in ashes on the mountainside,
the worries of mathematical problems,
nowhere to stop.

I opened again the old book
and read about the impossible ways
lessons travel through
the world's attention,
animated in the company
of mad characters.

In dreams about my schools I forget
my locker's combination of ages,
a lock parted with numbers,

opening signals on the wings
of a large, dusty moth
sleeping by my records,
by my radio long ago.

While I studied
I heard John Lennon
had been killed
on the street.

At the end of my dreams about cities
the buses drop off questions
for a traveler lost in old games
of speech and margins, strange
industry far from home.

Remind the rabbit's heart,
a watch, of faces
timed with the apple
trees of play and work
the songbirds ask to agree,
in the curious mouths
of the month of Alice,
September.

Assignment #1 - Megalomania

I don't want to be misunderstood when I talk of avoiding a journey, a search; I'm not saying no movement is necessary. I'm talking about the feeling I had most strongly in the period of my worst sickness, a feeling of always being on the verge of a great discovery, a revelation, of finding some wonderful answer, embodied in life, a transformation, a becoming, that would then hold and last forever, changing everything about me, and this was so tantalizing. But this feeling, this yearning, destroyed my ability to survive in the everyday world. It made simple decisions difficult.

The temporary discovery of another world often ended in fear and a sense of vast responsibility for the whole of life's distance, the future. A grand, terrible pressure would build up inside me and I knew I would fail my universal role; my megalomania left me crippled, emotionally and physically. There are traces, deep impressions also, of this mania inside me still, and I remain embarrassed and chagrined, and the shame and form and sense of this exposure to the world's eyes eats away at me gradually, slowly, I am afraid.

Sometimes I feel I have recovered, when I feel cozy, protected, surrounded by a sense of life as it once was, a sense of my old self, the limits of my world. Of course people weren't reading my thoughts, what a strange idea! I was just a kid, a person unknown to the vast conspiracy of dream life and eternity. No one was sharing my mind; my dreams were only my own dreams.

Even as I write this, or especially so, I hear voices answering me, making me stop and listen, making me wonder if it would be easier not to write or think at all. As soon as I seem to be complaining then the outside world has an answer, a response that leaves me worried I'm upsetting a fragile balance. And I easily can start seeing contradictions in what I say, or alternatives to my position, a position I can see as simplistic, or a stubborn holding on to an impossible, lost past, a denial of sensations that really are true, in a way, and real. The people from the world outside, and yet still inside my mind, answer with my own uncertainties. They ask, do you really want to return to that sense of isolation and youth, isn't that impossible, haven't you just been growing up? Are you afraid of the adult world?

Myra and the Woman on the Stock

On Hallowe'en, Myra wore
an ugly rubber mask to the back
office where forty women worked,
covering her broad, good face,
and that's how she felt:
front office broker, Mr. Stone
had told her,
fire three women,
you choose.

Inside Myra's cabinet,
a woman etched on a stock
certificate carried the earth
for anyone who bought her.

Mr. Stone liked the woman
and bought 20,000 shares.
He felt her each time he shuffled
his portfolio, each time he felt
his wife.

The day before he had bought another
20,000 of her and now Myra
counted the stock, watching the woman
who was actually a statue,
but who, long ago in Greece,
had once been alive,
standing for a sculptor.

After the woman stood for the sculptor
five hundred days, the statue
was tied to a cart.
As it was driven away, under the road
and the fields, hollows opened
in the shape of the woman's body,
a crowd of them
standing there, scattered,
as if women grown beneath the soil
had been drawn out like roots,
caverns remaining.

And then all that had fallen and gathered
around her in the courtyard when she stood
for the sculptor, all rock cut

from the woman, shards and splinters,
dust that had sifted into splits
in the flagstones and wrung from the cloth
that had wiped the marble,
all dirt first washed from her body,
skin that the weather had ground
and that the sculptor's palms
had lapped away, all slate
her feet had worn away,
the smell of the eucalyptus trees
and the way she smelled to the cat,
the taste of water and the sound
of the beetles, the sound of her legs shifting,
her memories of birds after they flew above her
and the way she had been seen by each bird,

all filled the hollows until the fields
fell away like cloth,
divulging hundreds of women, none alike.

The Archaeology of Nearby Parks

Out in the city all the children
are solving my mystery.
You heard my story too, long ago,
and built my leaf-box again,
below the park,
changing old anger into soil.

What I boil down to is familiar,
loss and sadness,
and then hope and love again,
layers of sediments, steeping green
tea for memory and forgetfulness.

I tried to create paper wheels,
devices for dreams turning a listener
in the moon, but my eyes faded
in the story,
my spoken words,
terrible relics
of confidence.

Sunlight fed time again, and the animals
walked with us on soft, frozen leaves,
secret water drying up to show
the trundle path of hidden life
growing through childhood.
After resting,
the rain brought the old place
sounds of thoughts.

Assignment #2 - Conspiracy

Again the sense of the hidden world of sight, inside vision, reaching from a sense of continuous, linked spaces, the spaces building from inside of each of our minds, becomes overwhelming as the areas the minds link, in a connection of chances, suddenly seem planned, predestined. This sense of planning, as if many other people know me from this hidden world, makes for a sense of conspiracy that never quite goes away, even with the reassurance of an otherwise caring, trusting peace of mind that holds me in an unusual and fascinating way, when the observation seems mutually kind and even naturally wonderful. This peace of mind can seem stronger than any fears the sense of conspiracy holds, the fear of the plan disappearing into a sense of completeness and sharing.

I still need my privacy, an inside and an outside, even if it is only a construction of my beliefs, a way to hide. I want to have an imagination. My own world of senses, my own thoughts, can remain true to me even with sharing and visits from others, who I imagine, yet just in case I remain cautious and always kind and accepting of the power of others, gaining permission to be myself, though I know that sounds odd and perhaps impossible to achieve.

Who is real, what version of the person do we see and sense? The invisible people crowd my mind's focus, over-lapping me with their images which become suddenly true, as real as my own sense of self, as they share my mind, moving with me, opening, closing, listening and shifting perspectives, until I lose my own perspective and share a new mind.

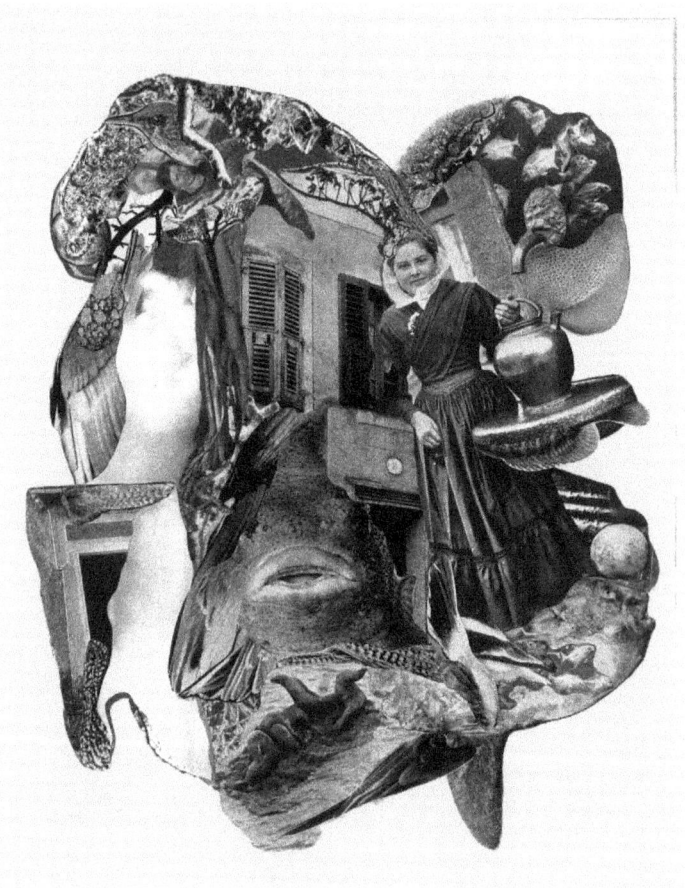

The Beginning Homecare Worker

My bicycle slopes corners together.
Paths circle the buildings flowering along
our stems, far away from us.
Our spokes, like bees,
whirling, ease eight pivots.

Sturdy wheels of air hold me
gathering loops,
long pathways working
poor, healthy roads.

Inside the rooms
windows open sunlight, wind flows
inside the sky faucets turn into
the watery floor, cleaning the earth.
Cloudy buckets empty and fill.
The common elements, vinegar, vegetable,
rags, clean strands
rinsing in streams.

Alfred, whose many gentle, odd
hammers and dollies had sculpted
fenders, pulled the splinter from my palm
I'd caught on the string mop's handle.

Slower, together, in separate rooms,
my sweeping, his eyes, his chair,
I stopped cleaning and felt my eyes had saddened.

Behind the kitchen in the house remaining
around his wife's room, Frank, 98,
wondered if his grandson would be called
toward Kuwait to fight again.

The trolley line ended across the hill
before the freeway filled the valley
below Mabel's window. She had connected
the telephone lines. She shows me how
to wind the thread three times
around the needle, securing the last stitch.

Almost fully, winds, leaves
green, dark playful sleep

work forms,
work forms grow
people, samples of life
giving the work form,
moving.

The choices furniture placed apart
grow familiar resting places,
like a cloth sail moving the room
around with us,
then motionless.

Privacy and curiosity divide into paths,
then join in the home,
to the city. Witnesses,
maps, hills appear,
layers of foliage.
Time, the moments opening
choices, the children's visits
visits of the children's children,
waiting. The moments and choices
are young still and crafty.

Following visits, almost as a young child,
toward these sturdy, knowledgeable people,
simple tasks held us.
Trust, like waiting for letters,
what have they opened,
what responses will change us
and add memory to accomplishments?

Pine needles layer the floor.
The days he became blind lengthen,
and the stroke.
Silly calls out from his bed,
a retired salesman who loves his wife,
and who doesn't have to worry
about moving the family again
or accepting school in the morning.
Caught in the soft, unwanted holiday,
he belongs outside where his car slowly lost
strength and dropped toward the useful
saws, elaborate wiring his sons empower now,
and wooden benches beneath the medicine room.

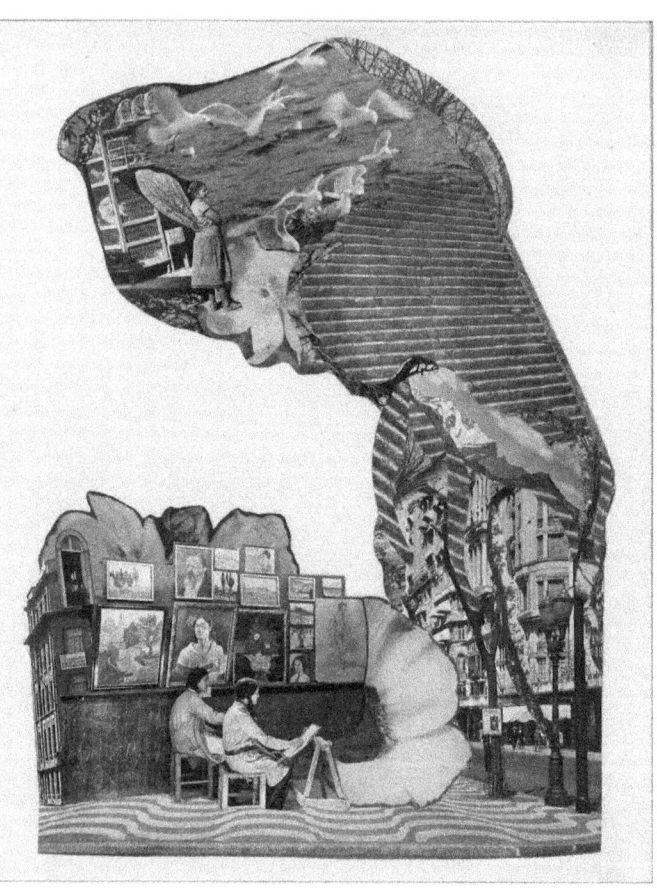

Strange Gardens, Companions

Listening shadows,
our hidden worlds
inside each other,
words in our eyes
became old letters,
flowers gone to seed
in the garden
hospital, opened
memory schedules
for the bees
and trains to spring.

Pelicans flew over the sand,
roots and twisting stems
of the wild strawberries
holding down the sandclocks,
breathing the past,
the car far away
across the dunes, the men

and women of the ocean
muffled inside sunlight.

A hummingbird
in the damp, fall
camellia blossoms,
by a window,
located our rooms
in unknown places outside,
for the always changing
dreams missing, gaining
portions of the night.

I remember the curious
passages in summer
letters collecting
in a world
of endless dreaming
where no one reaches home
before waking in the morning.

We walked by the herons
of the lake standing

near old garbage mounds,
now a sanctuary of poplars,
eagles, wild carrot,
swallows, chicory, a car
waiting to be recognized
by our dog.

Assignment #3 - Schizophrenia and Choice

So now I'm choosing my fate, as if I could choose how my imagination and spirit work to situate me in the public spaces of society, in the public mind and in the moral realm of the future in sight, all around us. Why do we doubt the ways of others? How do we know what each other feels, senses? Can we compare ourselves with each other confidently? Is there a common notion of getting along and cooperating for the general benefit of society?

It's difficult to know what people want and desire in details, in constructing reality for themselves and others. All this brings me to my old topics, to the notions of a private self, of individuality and the group, to boundaries and sensitivities, and when I start thinking about all of that I find myself certain, certain I am still crazy and confused and once again worried I am wrong, in an involuntary way often as if all of this world, this swirling life about me has caught me up in the energy of connections and has me in control even if I have choices to make, and whether or not I choose correctly, all this energy will act upon me freely anyway: the world will go on without me whether I am aware of it or not, just as I can't control my dreams.

My sense of magic, if I can call the connections and the world of the imagination, magic, is such a naïve, innocent version and that is why I am still worried about the competitions of the soul, the struggles of boundaries. There is a strange sense of danger even if one is only keeping alive safely, aware of the tenderness of life and not at all wanting anyone to come to harm, not knowingly harming anyone, not bringing pain or concerns of fear to anyone.

Yet we are always hurting each other, it seems, with misunderstanding; isn't it difficult for people to get along still? Of course. Even when so many want the best for each other there is strife and struggle. One thing seems certain: we can't all be friends, but isn't that what we all want the most? Maybe not. Maybe we want to decide, to choose, to select and review people, to build our lives carefully with careful decisions and prejudices and attitudes. We don't really want to be friends with everyone. And so then I think, yes, my imagination is faulty, my ways are strange, and yes, I am wrong, as I've arrived here, so strangely, and what is it that brought me here? How did this all happen, this becoming schizophrenic?

Can I still answer along with my treatment that it is just in my head, my brain, the chemicals, the faulty connections in my brain cause the strange connections in my life?

Yes, my medicines help; I know I still need help. I like being responsible, healthy and able to help my family and friends. I like taking care of myself and others.

What is the unruly imagination? What are dreams? How do we create beyond our reasoning, and where are we going?

Transcription from the Radio

The world began to change then,
an evolution of perspective,
obscured people with secret voices
hoping I would believe
the long sentence was true,
handed down from the beautiful,
fallible court,
the eerie cloisters,
the child's palace sleeping
in the shadows of my thoughts.
I listen to their opinions of time,
acoustical dreams I try to answer,
how my heart is tired.

    Are you still there? I am just getting old,
thinking haphazardly. Giulio Camillo built a
wooden memory theater in the 16th century,
shelter for the myriad, ancient stations
of Saturn, taught by elephants, and whales,
wearing Mercury's sandals.
    His view of heaven and knowledge would be
dismantled, innocent words auguring insomnia

and space travel, collapsing, harmony and
characters lingering above. The earth was their
children. Statues could speak of you in the city,
telescopes soon discovering the past.

Maybe you would know how the voices carry
in your own world.

A peaceful word comes down from the sky,
though I hear a mysterious story about demons
and angels of surveillance, who compare people,
every thought accounted for.

Long ago, my mother, father, sister, and our
cat couldn't foresee my future, time then to listen
to the radio, Pacifica's signal pulsing brightly in
the dark, people emerging with tentative eyes,
ideals, starting to watch me question myself.

Thelonious Monk was still alive, but silent, his
old recordings building free colleges of delight.
Science fiction writers leaked broadcasts to my
ear, and as I followed lessons of nighttime voices
clairaudience became seemingly true, a shy
energy imagining you, in the future. Some cities
prospered with logic and machine languages,

borrowing a fortune of light from others. We
were able to travel to Mexico in our car,
almost 50 years ago.

Once, we rode the train to Hermosillo, then
the bus to the sea and an empty blue sky. On the
quiet beach where we walked, my mother the
singer and maker of pottery traded our old box
camera for an ironwood carving of a bird, an
encounter with the only other person
I remember there, the woodcarver.

Alone in the sun I had no wishes to be
curious. I wheel this absence in my simple mind
in a round-about way, sending useless letters to
the small, open-windowed motel facing the sea
where the dolphins leap.

The dusty, black train rolls along through the
Sonoran desert, odd, original music playing from
one old speaker in a sleeping car, near a yellow
vase of fragrant gardenias.

Thelonious pauses by the piano and listens
for his friends to answer with their own refrains.
A melody travels home in a certain key, devoted
mysteriously.

Losing memory in an old city, loving
characters hear familiar voices on the radio,
in the face of a winter morning, all the work
in the past to create tomorrow saved up
like a smile, laughing again, records turning,
turtles carrying time back from a distant,
impossible land sinking into the sea.

A curious, glaucous star is blinking on the radio
tower.

The nighttime voices are speaking,
rhyming like a child,
yes, I hear them tell me,
we will let you go free,

air and water, sunshine and dreams,
poems in your garden help you reason,
strange amnesia startled by the bees.

The Newly Developed, Revolutionary Typewriter

This is the most solid machine
that was ever painted blue
and the blue is the most strong color
that a painter's arm brushed
the strongest arm
the strongest belly that balanced
the largest orange
that his strong wife refused to pick
off their wiry tree
she told him
pick your own fruit
I am not your worker,
husband, you live
in the new Cuba,
make your own lunch,
husband
and the strong worker
who painted the strong machine
the most clear and solid blue

thought about her words
as he ate his lunch
balancing his orange on his belly,
feet out before him
that clear, blue day
while the trucks and buses went by
past the hole he dug in the black ribbon
that circled the island.

Assignment #4 - Schizophrenia and Emptiness

It's surprising to me still how inconsistently my brain experiences the world of sounds, words, and pictures, and I am still unable to feel at ease exploring the emptiness of the world. This emptiness fills me and then I have the feeling of many people who fear they have lost themselves, lost their soul, their mind, that they are only made up of others, that others fill them and do what they please with us, even seeing impossibly far, or close, into our secrets and our words and thoughts as we grow dim and blank.

Slowly, though, I am growing accustomed to this emptiness and feeling of being shared by others, and most importantly I am trying to feel less ashamed of it, the emptiness at the heart of me, the sadness. So what if others move about and read my thoughts, my body, and my written words also? I don't feel as afraid as I used to. But I am feeling happy today so I can quickly write these words and fool myself. Yes, I am troubled but it is not the end of the world. But I am shocked at how brilliant they are, those interlopers and discoverers. I can't hide anything and the city fills with those who can escape, leaving the rest of us here with desires to belong though we are always just entering where the others are leaving. Yes, I am very ashamed of being schizophrenic because I suppose the thoughts of being wrong are belonging with my illness.

Why do schizophrenics feel observed and judged? Why has it taken me so long to identify with others like me? Because as I have said so often, I can't seem to face my illness alone, or as part of a group of similarly afflicted either, instead I feel everyone is just smarter and better adjusted, only they keep their secrets close. They care about us, about our illnesses, and don't want anxiety to spill over into their calm acceptance. Life is hard for all of us, they say. I want to belong but I always talk my way out of fondness. Yet I still feel so lucky and grateful and know things could be so much worse: I am adjusting to the invisible world.

The Biography of Uncommon Longing

I share my birthday with the artist Harry Smith,
a sentimental coincidence like my mother's own
overlapping with Harry, when both were young,
not knowing where each would travel,
or if they would return.

When strange characters try to solve questions
about work, I am charmed by their days and
valuable creations, afraid of what I might find in
the Biography of Uncommon Longing.

Listening to songs, talking, reading letters and
books, impressions form in light and shadows,
people we begin to see and hear, leafing through
our memory, as the years go by, sympathetic
chapters and company.

Our chronology starts working in the spirit
world, calling them toward us, Mother and Father
Time presiding, reaching for us in the archives,
illuminating our eyes.

These libraries though stay open in dreams, and
often I forget who I am, so I ask the spirits, do you
also consider us and our attention?

We keep each other alive, building this world
together.

Harry Smith collected old records of folk
music, revealing ancient geometric patterns
in the fiddler's sunshine, banjos and guitars,
voices.

In his world, children play with string figures,
patterns in the eye of the beholder, Easter eggs,
paper airplanes and butterflies.

I have read that he rode his bicycle from
Bellingham to the dances of the Lummi Tribe,
recording the chants and drums on acetate discs,
seeing how the ancestors moved in the dancing,
and noting the beauty of the ceremonial language.

The tribe trusted Harry to transcribe details
in notebooks, and one was saved, in the Burke
Museum, but he lost many others.

In 1943 and 1944 he studied anthropology at
the University, while my young mother attended
classes there.

Helen also worked as a stenographer at Boeing,
quickly transcribing facts of commerce and flight.
Swing dancing in the dancehalls late into the

night, she slept on the trains home, her future
uncertain, her brilliance running ahead of her
like a white blossom on the forehead of a deer
escaping into the forest.

There is no evidence the two met one day
on campus among the old herb beds, under
the sequoia. A fledgling heron waited above,
wondering whether to fly into the open, wooded
theater across the lawn, the young sorcerer saying,
don't be afraid, you will live a very long time,
and always be listening for songs in the gardens
outside.

April, and thoughts of May, write this poem,
my mother living not too far away, Opening
Memory at the Lilac Window.

Unable to escape captivity, people hope a way
to remember who they are will be found together,
like the location of dreams.

In a dark, blue dream of unexpected journeys,
my mother's memory of two miscarriages and a
third child who only lived a short while, asked
questions of the earth at night, perennials
underground, prayers of the garden.

My sister and I were lucky to be born, clay vessels lined with Japanese Gift Calligraphy, uncovered in the tumultuous city, far from paradise.

Searching the ruins, the Ancient Librarians could hear my mother singing, her art then balancing the morning of the green bicycle she rode toward our school, looking around the neighborhood.

Somewhere ahead, the spirits of the pages were reading the gossip of the ages in a nestled State of Being, the imagination of life hearing things, informing us of love.

In my bewilderment, on a long walk, I am bordered with antique thistles and angels, a gothic motif I tend like a clock of twigs, and forebodings, in my mother's 95th year, after visiting each other, though often we are silly.

I say to myself, how good to hold her hand again and sit in the garden, after this long year, but she wants to fix a tiny tear in the center of my voice.

Her wisdom hides from me, then appears as she looks into my eyes, and says, "You can go home now."

I need a peaceful place to ruminate, the flight
of thoughts between so many making these
designs, like flowers, to enchant me, a man
wondering why I become so cold, like a cabbage
growing in the lingering day, my babbling, the
way these notions travel, and the spirit world
unravels.

Someone in the dream talks about me, as if
he has all the time in the world, observing my
foibles, making notes in the different regions of
my brain.

Ensconced in an old tower, built long ago near
fields of lentils, he saves time like crabapple seeds,
or the whispering of bees, in a secret, or is he
telling one, transcribing ordinary moments
for scrupulous reasons?

When I am most happy, he may be away,
looking for others to console in the land of the
sleeping oats and blueberries.

Eating oats each morning at home I wait for
our blueberries to ripen and many other flowers
appear in our garden, small, beautiful utensils
reaching the world for a short while, oddly made
from what they touch and taste, and what touches

them, sky, sun and rain, made of colors, blue
nigella, maroon and lace astrantia, dark iris, and
the yellow phlomis spires.

I am reading again, after pausing to look up at
the pink clouds.

These libraries though stay open in dreams,
and often I forget who I am.

From the Paper Mills

1.

With beeswax, she threads a needle, her gnarled fingers keeping the lore of human kindness, and sews on the button. I wonder about the world she will mend next, sailing ships and clouds in the distance, and where the book begins, long lines of clouds and words, tattered and mended. When we emptied the sewing drawer she saved spools of thread, needles, odds and ends, and I took a strange chunk of beeswax home with me, old, darkened, unpolished facets, that had belonged to her father, the tailor, Michael Twardoski. What if, in a rosy, theatrical interlude, he sewed the secret insignias of tigers, giants, beavers, oaks, bees, and seals, on baseball uniforms for Polish acrobats and musicians, in the era of paper mills, long ago, in our dreams, where we are all seeking comfort and joy this season. . .

Uniforms and fields still appear so vividly colored on the Minor League baseball cards, Obak Tobacco, T212, from 1910 and 1911, pink and yellow, white and maroon clouds in the blue sky around the players, from Tacoma, Seattle, Portland, Spokane. My grandfather could have first imagined the clothes he made, memories working in his own cloud factory, a small store of patterns and scissors, lamps, in Buckley, Washington.

BURNS, Tacoma, N. W. L.   LEARD, Seattle, N. W. L.   WEED, Spokane, N. W. L.

Ancient factories of paper, Chinese, Arab, then European, fed by the rag merchants, women sorting through the soiled heaps, children cleaning the cold vats at night, remember for us, elaborating the plans in our heads, on paper of all colors, languages, numbers, and music finding space to breathe.

HUNT, SACRAMENTO, P. C. L.   FLATER, OAKLAND, P. C. L.   ADAMS, VANCOUVER, N. W. L.

Conspiracies of tobacco smoke cure so briefly the
loss of stamina and pleasure, the help some workers
need for such hours. Indians chew coca leaves in the
Andes, hoisting the great weights of darkness in the
silver mines, with the Wobblies and longshoremen,
near the lumber mills, and now in the vast, fortified
warehouses, workers of the computer age.

The history books get jumbled together, pages flying
backward, family trees, wings of birds and little names,
baseball clouds over the fields harmlessly floating in
the fibers, halftones, chromolithographs, behind por-
traits and the batting stances of heroes for the children
to save, the fielders as tough as nails, immigrants who

maybe would sail back to Europe soon, to fight in the poisonous War, like my grandfather did. I never met him and no one told me any stories about the battles he fought.

One document reveals he sailed back to America on August 14, 1919, from Brest, France, after two years, a foot soldier with an eighth grade education, Private 1st Class, in Company H, 30th Infantry. 26 years old, he had been learning the art of making clothes when he enlisted, not yet a citizen. He may have had time to see the Mona Lisa in Paris before returning, still in uniform, savoring the peacefulness and mysterious good luck to be alive, one afternoon, standing before the most famous portrait of all.

He married my grandmother, Mary Gutowski, in Tacoma, and then they moved to a little house on the rural Enumclaw road, before settling in Buckley, nearby, where their daughter and sons could visit the library.

When my mom was a girl, a rough, older boy tried to kiss her in the Sweet Shop, the tip of his cigarette burning her skin. I wish some of the joy inventing ice cream brought to the world could heal her memory, like rainwater finally ending a terrible fire.

2.

In a book published in 1918, the Parisian poet and soldier, Guillaume Apollinaire de Kostrowitzky, wrote that cigarettes were "as bitter and delicious as life." Riding a train to the Front, he had fallen in love with a girl sharing his compartment, and would write enthusiastic letters and poems about the War, but soon he became sad again, the clamor and glorified scenes fading like the dreams of a madman unafraid of anything. Injured in the trenches by flying shrapnel while reading a newspaper, he died at 38 in Paris, his adopted city. Creating myths for the city of art, the alluring light of his words, taken down into the street, made odd leaps of associations like acrobats in courtyards where drunkards and gnostic secretaries recorded the colors on posters at dusk. Detectives had accused him of stealing the Mona Lisa, after the painting disappeared from the Louvre one day in 1911, and even his friend Picasso wouldn't defend him. Apollinaire was imprisoned, suffering trials of humiliation. Paris had taken his surreal key to the sky, poems of the new aeroplanes, thousands of birds flocking around the great aviator, Christ, in the city of catalogues, billboards, and windows.

3.

Strangers who never knew the old ballplayers saved their cards, as the collections of paper changed hands over the century, gaining great value, tobacco cards boys had once begged for outside the smoke shops, advertisements meant to stiffen the cigarette packs, cards that became charms in a burgeoning world. Addicted to the colors, forms, and faces, and the idea of baseball encapsulated in the small pictures, the boys were never satisfied until they had played all day in the baseball universe, but there was work to do.

COLEMAN, TACOMA, N. W. L.   WIGGS, OAKLAND, P. C. L.   FULLERTON, PORTLAND, P. C. L.

Before I knew about baseball, I drew pictures in pencil of soldiers in uniforms holding rifles and wearing hats and caps, copying them awkwardly from a forgotten encyclopedia. A part of me soon abandoned these innocent sketches along with my fascination with toy guns, or guns of any kind, but sometimes, in boredom, an absence of imagination, the curiosity returned. What I needed were trowels, rakes, a walking stick to carry, or wooden spoons, an oboe, or a French horn.

Finding a very quiet second grader in 1968 ready to listen, a beautiful quartet entered our house, the young musicians of Sgt. Pepper's Lonely Hearts Club Band looking out from the crowded, glowing collage on the record sleeve, wearing brightly colored uniforms of their own, holding musical instruments. I didn't know they all smoked marijuana cigarettes and their elaborate music was called psychedelic, considered indulgent, baroque, innovative, perhaps the most wonderful and popular record ever made. Their songs seemed peaceful to me, harmonious, rhythmic and healing for lonely children whose parents might be suffering from unbearable sadness, who might be lost in the large, hectic world of violence, turmoil, and separation, unable to talk about their troubles. I've never stopped listening to this music for long.

My family stayed together, barely, isolated and keeping secrets, but still sharing the outlook of many around us, the spirit of the age. We joined marches or parades in Washington, D.C. and San Francisco, for Peace, the beguiling idea that seemed better to me than War. I was just a kid, of course, who loved wearing a button with a peace sign, feeling shy but close to the energy of the large crowds of interesting people singing and walking along, hopeful our timeless goal would be reached someday, not with an apotheosis, but in small actions, and seasons, or as Pete Seeger always said, by moving a hill of sand slowly, a teaspoon at a time.

These people were also scholars, teachers, students, with many reasons for dissent as well as strong emotions, and many of them were Vietnam Vets, knowing the forces slamming against them. My recollections are innocent, and I remember a sense of warmth among strangers, and festivity, but maybe the urgency and pain of the adults touched me more than I know. I'm surprised no one took me aside later and said, "Don't be so naïve, we'll always have wars."

4.

I discovered a little magazine called The Trader Speaks, where people offered baseball cards of all kinds for sale, but I could only dream of acquiring the rare ones, like the Brown Backgrounds, T207, from 1912, depicting portraits with almost Parisian loveliness, the players appearing to wear makeup, rouge and powdered cheeks, soft eyes, like dancers or acrobats ready to leap over second base.

Travelling with my father into Los Angeles one afternoon on the bus to an old store near Fairfax, a cluttered place stuffed with paper ephemera, we bought a card of the old player I admired the most, the Brooklyn Dodger, Jackie Robinson, a 1956 Topps, a talisman my father could give me because this card was still affordable then. It would be worth hundreds of dollars now, but foolishly I sold it, with the rest of my little collection, when I was 21, before travelling by myself to South America. I've always regretted losing the card of Jackie Robinson, the most heroic ballplayer in history, though I am glad I was able to travel, because it turned out to be the last chance I had to see the world before events caught up with me.

Apollinaire had always looked far in his poems, even toward Vancouver B.C. and the Pacific Northwest, imagining the distant corner of the globe where my grandfather had arrived, 17 years old, in 1908, from Poland. The wireless telegraph connected the continents, but most people had to dream of the cities far away, putting together images from the newspapers, and books, imagination working in their own small factories, making and storing pictures and exotic conversations in the New World.

5.

The intrepid daughter, Helen Twardoski, would leave Seattle in 1947, and sail to Japan to work with a group of young women in the accounting office of the Occupying Government in Tokyo, staying for almost three years, making lifelong friends. Desolate ghost of the atomic clouds, sifting the ashes, could you find hope my mom and her friends were innocent emissaries, offering their good will where they travelled, a slight turn of the cycle, though the orders to drop the bombs came from their leaders?

My mom married my father in 1956, in New York City, the same year my grandfather died. My parents had met in Greenwich Village, far from home. Her younger brother, Richard, had stayed in Buckley and with my aunt Jan turned his father's tailor shop into a cleaners, though they still mended the clothes. Long ago, when reality and time were dissolving all around me, like the clouds and shadows on tobacco cards swirling into small dots and lines, like a lost soul, I visited my uncle, travelling south from Seattle on the bus.

Exploring the countryside, one afternoon I took a walk on the backroads around the grounds of the old Custodial School for the disabled, an ominous labyrinth I was unfamiliar with, surrounded by empty fields and isolated houses. That night as I slept I felt tremors, my body and brain shaking, as shocks of something like electricity passed through my spirit, wave after wave. I awoke unharmed in the morning, feeling oddly peaceful and placid. In the small room next to where I had slept I noticed a book by Pierre Teilhard de Chardin on my uncle's shelf, and I remembered this interesting name. When I returned home I began wondering about the importance of Teilhard's book for my uncle, who is a Catholic, a thoughtful, expressive man, who worked hard all of his life, and played the fiddle, always loving folk music, filled with joy. Over the years I heard a few stories about Teilhard, here and there, but always delayed investigating further.

A Jesuit and a scientist, he died in New York City in 1955, before his writings were published. He described a "noosphere," a mingling of all the thoughts on earth, sewing together all languages and cultures, plants and animals, the sky and clouds, evolving until the earth became conscious, one telepathic sphere, all beings joined in one mind.

My uncle is now a great grandfather, who likes to sit in the garden, who listens to music, a little withdrawn from the world, and I am unsure how to communicate with him. I am still probably an atheist, much like my parents, and I can become afraid of the unifying spheres of the theologians, overwhelmed by spirits questioning my inner life, dreams, memories, our place on earth.

Do we have eternal souls? How do we picture ourselves, as others see us? Where are the essential portraits stored? Tailors around the world had cards of their own to be saved by strangers. Individual portraits can merge with machines, sewing together costumes of nationalities, but official identity cards are not very artful.

The old Singer sewing machines pictured with the tailors of different nations are beautiful, advertisements of 1892, but my grandfather would wear new clothes in America. Each machine was different and the costumes recalled the old customs. Are souls only how we picture ourselves changing? The portrait of Mona Lisa may last forever. Will we be lost in the clouds, or in the phonics of our childhood? In youthful clothes, or the body of old age, as our faces reappear in all our relations. . .

CYRENE.

OVER.

CHINA.

OVER.